I Am Queen the Dreamer:
a story about starting a business

by Jasmine Furr

Illustrated by Ashleigh Sharmaine & Designed by Adam Hopkins

ISBN 978-1-7331667-1-3
Library of Congress Control Number: 2019912193

Untraditional Publishing Company, LLC
St. Louis, MO
orders@theachieversbooks.com

UNTRADITIONAL
PUBLISHING CO.

Every day when Queen wakes up,
she sees her parents and, with so much love,
they give her a list of sentences to say
to prepare her for an amazing day:
"I am smart!"
"I am brave!"
"I am happy!"
"I am great!"
"I am Queen the Dreamer and today is my day!"

QUEEN

So, Queen went to class to share a dream.
She made a speech on what she wants to be.
She said, "I want a website for an online store
where I'll sell shirts, books, and so much more.
I will sell them online and in the mall."
Her classmates said, "We will buy them all."
"We love the colors! We love the art."
"I did it." Queen said, "I am smart!"

Queen

At lunchtime, Queen sat with her friends King, Duke, and Allison.

Her classmate, Ace, walked up to them and asked the group, "May I join in?"

"No!" Duke said, "You can't sit with us."

"Listen!" Queen said, "That's unjust."

QUEEN

"Let's agree to be kind to others
and treat our classmates like our brothers.
Whether in class or during lunch,
Ace, you can always sit with us."
Ace sat down. His new spot was saved.
"Because," Queen said, "I am brave!"

Queen

During recess, Queen stood in line
to play jump rope one more time.
With every jump, they spelled her name.
She even played clapping games.
She had such fun jumping and clapping.
"I love recess." Queen said, "I am happy!"

10

Queen

After her classes, Queen went to band
with sheet music and flute in hand.
She never played before this year,
but she plays every week without fear.
Today was the band's afterschool show.
Queen played the flute in her first solo.
Her classmates cheered. Everyone was amazed.
"We did it." Queen said, "I am brave."

12

Queen

Queen went home for family dinner
at 6:00 p.m. and not a minute later.
She said, "I want to launch my website."
Her parents replied, "We'll do it tonight!"
Queen said, "Thank you for believing in me!
My dream is coming true. I am happy!"

Queen

Queen jumped online to start her website.
She added fun words and colors that were bright.
After creating links and writing code
her website was done and ready to go!
People bought shirts, books and so much more.
Everyone loved her online store.
Her parents were smiling. It was a great start.
"Awesome!" Queen said, "I am smart!"

Queen

16

Queen's friends and family came over to play
to celebrate such an amazing day.
Queen said, "All of the sentences came true."
"Great!" they said, "What did you do?"
Queen replied,
"I went to school, and I did great.
I saved a seat for my classmate.
At recess, I played with my friends.
I had my first solo in band.
I ate dinner with my family
and launched my online business for all to see."

"My entire day was as great as me!
Can you believe all that I achieved?
In just one day, I can say:
'I am smart!'
'I am brave!'
'I am happy!'
'I am great!'
I did all of this because I believed!
I did all of this because I am me!"

Queen